Blockchain Technology Simplified:

The Complete Guide to Blockchain Management, Mining, Trading and Investing in Cryptocurrency

Legal & Disclaimer

The information contained in this book and its contents is not designed to replace or take the place of any form of medical or professional advice; and is not meant to replace the need for independent medical, financial, legal or other professional advice or services, as may be required. The content and information in this book has been provided for educational and entertainment purposes only.

The content and information contained in this book has been compiled from sources deemed reliable, and it is accurate to the best of the Author's knowledge, information, and belief. However, the Author cannot guarantee its accuracy and validity and cannot be held liable for any errors and/or omissions. Further, changes are periodically made to this book as and when needed. Where appropriate and/or necessary, you must consult a professional (including but not limited to your doctor, attorney, financial advisor or such other professional advisor) before using any of the suggested remedies, techniques, or information in this book.

Upon using the contents and information contained in this book, you agree to hold harmless the Author from and against any damages, costs, and expenses, including any legal fees potentially resulting from the application of any of the information provided by this book. This disclaimer applies to any loss, damages or injury caused by the use and application, whether directly or indirectly, of any advice or information presented, whether for breach of contract, tort, negligence, personal injury, criminal intent, or under any other cause of action.

You agree to accept all risks of using the information presented inside this book.

You agree that by continuing to read this book, where appropriate and/or necessary, you shall consult a professional (including but not limited to your doctor, attorney, or financial advisor or such other advisor as needed) before using any of the suggested remedies, techniques, or information in this book.

Table of Contents

Introduction

Are you feeling weird about not having any idea about cryptocurrency? Are you confused with the concept of Bitcoin and blockchain? Do you think the concepts are too technical and that they go over your head? Are you finding yourself in a world of jargons and technical terms when it comes to cryptocurrency? If you are nodding your head for a "YES" to at least one of the above-mentioned questions, then not to worry - you have got hold of the right book.

Cryptocurrency is a digital currency that has no physical form in the real world. Bitcoin is the first cryptocurrency and the most popular of other digital currencies in the digital market. All these digital currencies run on blockchain technology which is a decentralized peer-to-peer network making the transactions transparent and secure at the same time.

Through the course of the book, we are intending to discuss understanding the concept of cryptocurrency, the blockchain technology it runs on, the most popular cryptocurrency – Bitcoin, the process of mining a Bitcoin and the basic guidelines to invest and trade in cryptocurrencies. Here is a quick snapshot of what is covered in the book:

- Reasons that led to invention of cryptocurrency
- Cryptocurrency, its history, and the work process
- Necessity of miners
- Properties of cryptocurrencies
- Most popular cryptocurrencies
- Background of blockchain technology

1

- Blockchain, its work process and the various features it holds
- Potential applications where blockchain technology can be used
- Bitcoin and its base technology
- Ways to buy and sell Bitcoins
- Things to be done before purchasing a Bitcoin
- Places to find Bitcoins
- Bitcoins & its characteristics
- Disadvantages of Bitcoins
- Mining process
- Complexity in mining – 'Proof of work.'
- Bitcoin mining difficulty
- Bitcoin mining hardware used by miners
- Bitcoin cloud mining
- Trading and investing in Cryptocurrency
- Risks and Regulations in trading or investing
- Mistakes to be avoided while trading cryptocurrency
- Investing cryptocurrency

A Word from the Author

I would like to take this opportunity to thank you for purchasing this book: "Blockchain Technology Simplified: The Complete Guide to Blockchain Management, Mining, Trading and Investing in Cryptocurrency."

When you rewind the accomplishments in the financial sector this year and segregate all the buzz that happened with respect to transactions in the digital world, you will often come across terms like "cryptocurrency," "Bitcoins," "blockchain technology," "Ethereum," "IOTA," etc. If you are a novice to this subject, I am sure these terms will have played on your mind. To better understand, you would have read articles that carry information about the rise of cryptocurrency mining farms in the global market, Bitcoin gaining popularity as a reliable cryptocurrency, skyrocketing Bitcoin valuation, etc. and will have wondered what it is all about.

These buzzwords have taken the Internet by storm and have forced many of us to do a bit of research to understand these terms. But unfortunately, despite its growing popularity, many of us still don't understand the concept of cryptocurrency, Bitcoin or blockchain technology. Even when we tend to read through the different blogs and articles, it all seems too technical with financial jargons that sound Greek and Latin.

"An investment in knowledge always pays the best interest."

Let us follow the quote above and try to understand the basics of this new financial concept and the underlying reason behind its "gaining popularity." In this book, we will be discussing in detail all about cryptocurrency, Bitcoin and blockchain technology. The chapters will serve as a beginner's guide to understanding the basic concepts of mining, trading and investing in cryptocurrency.

I hope this book will help you understand the concept of digital money and the ways in which it can be traded and invested digitally. Thank you once again for purchasing this book. I hope this book serves as an informative and exciting read for you!

Chapter One: Cryptocurrency

What is cryptocurrency? Is it the money of the future? Or is it something to do with digital transactions? These questions keep buzzing in our heads more than often when we get to hear these financial jargons. Cryptocurrency is now a global phenomenon, which is confusing to most people. There are still few governments, banks and financial institutions that seem to be unaware of its importance in the ever-evolving digital world.

Cryptocurrency was a side product of another invention by an unknown entity named Satoshi Nakamoto (an individual or a group of individuals) in early 2009. He announced about this new development, which was a "peer to peer electronic system" by the name Bitcoin. Though he never intended to invent a new currency, Bitcoin officially became the first cryptocurrency in the digital world and is still considered to be the most crucial cryptocurrency.

What Led to This Invention?

To understand this, let us discuss how our current conventional digital money works. All of us are aware that our current conventional digital money solely works on a payment network with accounts, transactions and balances. There is a regulatory body or a central authority responsible for governing the entire network to ensure all the transactions that happen are legitimate.

The ultimate aim of this body is to prevent double spending.

What is double spending? When an entity spends the same amount twice, it is called as double spending.

What do we understand from the above? All of these transactions are nothing but entries made on a central ledger, which is governed by a single body. The loophole we find in this system is that all the entities or participants are entirely dependent on this authority and place their trust in this third party.

Exploitations for personal gain or various other events can always happen. The journey to find a solution to this loophole led to another incredible path along with the intended path. The "Peer to Peer electronic system" was the intended path and the birth of cryptocurrency was the "other incredible path." This peer-to-peer electronic cash system was known as Bitcoin.

The entire process of cryptocurrency has been decentralized, i.e., the process of verifying the legitimacy of the transactions made has been distributed to every single entity in the payment network. In this way, you don't need to put your faith in a third-party but can operate with the absolute consensus of all peers.

But how does this absolute consensus happen? What if one or more peers disagree? This is where the blockchain technology comes into the picture. We will discuss in detail the blockchain technology in the next chapter. But first, let's understand the concept of cryptocurrency.

What is Cryptocurrency?

We all know that there is fiat currency and non-fiat currency, but what is the difference between the two? When a currency's value is determined and established by a government body, it is called "fiat currency." The currencies of various countries, such as the dollars, euros, pounds, yen, rupees, etc., fall under this category. The "non-fiat currency" is not determined by the government body but backed by other physical bodies, which have value on the market. 'Gold' will fall into this category. What makes it valuable? The limited quantity and the increase in demand for gold!

Cryptocurrency falls somewhere in between fiat and non-fiat currency. It is not backed by a physical quantity; although, most of the world's governing bodies have recognized it to be a legal stock.

Cryptocurrency is a digital currency that uses an encrypted format to verify transactions and generate money. This encrypted format is called cryptography. The transactions made during the process are added to a public ledger known as the 'Transaction blockchain.' The system that manages this transaction and approves the same creates new coins (Bitcoins) through the mining process.

To explain in simpler terms – Cryptocurrencies are limited digital entries in a database, which no one can modify, or change without following specific conditions. Compare this to your bank account! Your bank accounts are nothing but entries in a database that can be modified based on specific conditions such as a credit or debit entry made to your account. When you consider it, you get to understand that money in the digital world is nothing but verified entries in databases related to accounts, balances or transactions.

History of Cryptocurrency

BitGold was the first decentralized digital cryptocurrency, which was introduced by Nick Szabo between 1998 and 2005. It is also said that 'e-gold' was developed in 1996 even before BitGold took its place. The predecessor of Bitcoin is BitGold.

Satoshi Nakamoto published a paper called, 'Bitcoin: A Peer-to-Peer Electronic Cash System' in 2008. After this, Bitcoin went public in 2009 and officially became the first decentralized digital coin.

Until January 2015, there were more than 500 different types of cryptocurrencies, but only ten of them had market capitalization close to ten million dollars. Even though there are other cryptocurrencies like Ethereum, Bitcoin is the most commonly known and used cryptocurrency on the digital market. The total market capital of cryptocurrencies reached 600 billion dollars in December 2017.

How Do They Work?

Cryptocurrencies work on the P2P (Peer to Peer) technology. It consists of a network of peers where each peer will have a record of the complete transactional history to help balance every account connected to it. Let us try to understand it better with an example:

Alisha gives ten Bitcoins (a form of cryptocurrency) to Sam. The whole network will know about this transaction in a few seconds, but the confirmation of the transaction happens only after a specific amount of time.

The critical concept in cryptocurrency is, "this confirmation." Until the time the transaction is confirmed, it is in the pending status.

Once the confirmation is made, there is no going back – it cannot be reversed, forged or modified. This transaction now becomes a part of the existing historical transactions called 'blockchain.'

So, who confirms this transaction? Miners. It is the job of the miners to confirm the transaction in a cryptocurrency network. What do they do? They check the transactions, confirm them as 'legitimate' and send them to the entire network.

Once the miner confirms the transaction, every other node connected to the network will have to add it to its database, which in turn becomes a part of the blockchain. The miners get rewarded for this job in the form of Bitcoins. The activity of the miners is the most vital part of the entire cryptocurrency network.

Why Do They Need Miners?

Since we are dealing with a decentralized network, which has no central authority for the task to be entrusted upon; the cryptocurrency will need a specific kind of mechanism to prevent one party in power from abusing it.

What if one party creates thousands of peers and spreads fraudulent transactions? The entire system would collapse, which is why miners are needed to get this done.

Miners will have to find the hash program (a cryptographic functional product), which connects the new block with its predecessor that is called "proof of work." In Bitcoin, the 'proof of work' is based on SHA 256 Hash algorithm. There is no need to worry if you don't know the details of this specific algorithm. All you need to understand is – this algorithm can be some cryptographic puzzle, which the miners compete to solve.

Once the miner finds the required solution, he can add the new block to the existing blockchain. This will give him the authority to add another transaction that helps to give him a specific number of Bitcoins as an incentive for his work.

This process creates valid Bitcoins, and there is no other alternative way other than the said method. Miners will have no other choice but to solve this cryptographic puzzle to create Bitcoins.

Only a specific amount of cryptocurrency tokens can be formed in a specific time due to the complexity of the cryptography puzzles. The strong point in this whole concept of decentralization is this process where no one in the network has the ability to break the consensus.

Cryptocurrencies are built on cryptography (strong encryption format), which is secured by mathematics. Only if the miners solve this mathematical problem, they'll be able to gain access to the Bitcoin address. This way the entire process is completely secured.

If you are ready to invest in your computer's processing power to solve the cryptographic puzzles and confirm the transaction and create Bitcoins, then you can be a miner.

Mining is the procedure to solve the cryptographic puzzles to create Bitcoins or other cryptocurrencies, and the people who do this are called miners. Dozens of Bitcoins were mined about 7 – 8 years ago, using a couple of GPUs (Graphics Processing Units), but now you will need a tailor-made ASIC mining rig to get a small portion of a Bitcoin.

Properties of Cryptocurrencies

Most of the cryptocurrencies share quite a common set of properties, but they cannot be defined by a specific rules or procedures.

Monetary properties:

- Limited supply

The schedule written in the code restricts the supply of the tokens in most cryptocurrencies, i.e., you can calculate the future monetary supply of a cryptocurrency today based on the current supply of the tokens. In Bitcoin, the final supply will be reached sometime in the year 2140 as the supply of tokens decreases in time.

- Only bearers

Cryptocurrencies are similar to coins of gold as cryptos are represented by themselves. They can be called digital gold. They don't represent debts like your fiat money in bank accounts.

Transactional properties:

- Fast

Transactions happen in an instant on the network, and it hardly takes a couple of minutes to receive the confirmation. There is no physical representation of the location, and everything happens in the network globally.

- More secure

Public key cryptography system is used to lock all the cryptocurrencies, and only the owner of the private key can send these digital currencies. Strong cryptography and the magic of mathematics make it difficult to hack this system.

- Not connected to the real world

None of the transactions or accounts is connected to the real world. You receive Bitcoins on 'some address that has 30 characters to it.' Though you can analyze the transaction flow, you can never find the real world identity of the user's address that had sent you the Bitcoins.

- Not reversible

Once a transaction is confirmed, it can never be reversed. Once you send the money, it means you have sent it; there are no means of reversing it even if you had sent it to a scammer by mistake or if it has been stolen from your computer by some hacking software. There is a bit of safety concern in this area.

Most Popular Cryptocurrencies

The following are the most popular cryptocurrencies in the market as on today:

- Bitcoin

- Ethereum

- Ripple

- Ethereum classic

- Litecoin

- Monero

- NEM

- Angur

- Dash

- Waves

Will This New Digital Currency Last Long?

The value of cryptocurrencies is still unpredictable with sudden rapid growth and sudden low tides, but this digital currency doesn't seem to be slowing down. Many countries have taken a positive standpoint towards this digital currency and the new wave it has been creating.

The rapidly increasing environment of the digital transactions will force cryptocurrencies to rule the digital world soon. All said and done, the true power of this digital currency lies in the hands of the common people. If everybody plunges into this area and start investing in cryptocurrency, the future might see immense growth in the value of cryptocurrencies like that of 'gold.' Because both these non-fiat currency is limited in supply thereby increasing their core value.

Chapter Two: Blockchain Technology

In the last chapter, you got a basic idea about the concept of cryptocurrency and how it works. For the cryptocurrency to function, you will need technology to make it work, and that technology is "Blockchain technology." We will be getting into the details of blockchain technology and the popular cryptocurrency – Bitcoin. Technically speaking, Bitcoin is powered by the blockchain technology. Since this book will be dealing with Bitcoin as the cryptocurrency, we will henceforth be using only the term "Bitcoin" instead of using the common term "cryptocurrency" to avoid confusion.

Background of Blockchain Technology

Now that we have already understood that Bitcoin is the first cryptocurrency in the digital world that is completely decentralized, we will get into details of how blockchain technology works and understand the basic features it carries.

The blockchain technology is a distributed public ledger that uses a hash algorithm for anonymity, proof of work for accurate maintenance and incentives for validating the transactions.

Blockchain technology needs to be implemented for the above features to work in synchronization. A detailed orientation is given below:

- The blockchain is the distributed public ledger that helps in storing all the transactions that have happened in the history of Bitcoin. You don't have a central ledger; instead, every single entity in the network will have a copy of the ledger. This ledger keeps getting updated across all the nodes every time a transaction is made in the network. If any single entity tries to make a forged change in the ledger, it would be flagged as 'corrupt.'

- Though every single entity will be able to see the transaction, nobody will know the identity of the account. This happens because anything and everything stored in the blockchain is encrypted using a hash algorithm to ensure anonymity. Hash algorithms cannot be decrypted because even a minute change in the input will produce an entirely different hash that is no way related to the original algorithm.

- The transactions that happen can be confirmed and maintained only when a complex cryptographic puzzle called "proof of work" is solved. A hash target value is designated to every block (data).

- Around 250 (this is the usual count) unverified Bitcoin transactions are clubbed together into one block by the miners. They try to compute its hash and compete with the other miners to find a set of specific characters called Nonce. The total hash value obtained from the hash of the earlier block, the transaction data and the Nonce have to match with the final target hash value (which is pre-assigned). Block = Hash + Block data + Nonce.

- When the miners successfully validate the transactions, they would receive incentives in the form of Bitcoins. This process is called "Bitcoin mining." The miners are rewarded with 12.5 BTC per block, which is approximately $34380. It takes around ten minutes on an average for each block to mine. Bitcoin is also represented as BTC.

If you successfully mine a block, you earn a whopping amount in minutes. But it is not an easy feat as it takes an average of about 12 billion laptops to work in parallel to achieve this!

What is Blockchain?

A public distributed database that has encrypted ledgers is called blockchain. A 'block' records the recent transaction and is the 'present-day entry which gets added to the existing blockchain.' It gains its permanence once it is verified and becomes an indefinite part of the blockchain.

"Blockchain will do to technology what the Internet did to communication." – Ginni Rometty, CEO of IBM.

When Satoshi Nakamoto first released Bitcoin in 2008, it just said – "It is a peer to peer electronic cash system which helps to enable 'online transactions to be done directly without the need of an intermediary.' This P2P electronic cash system was named Bitcoin."

Though this new digital currency created waves, it was the technology that was used by this Bitcoin that created excitement in everyone. This technology is known as the blockchain technology, and Bitcoin is just an application that uses this technology. Several other applications run on blockchain technology.

The FT Technology reporter, Sally Davies said,

"Blockchain is to Bitcoin, what the Internet is to email. It is a big electronic system, on top of which you can build applications. Currency is just one such application."

This technology helps in creating the complete record of transactions that is maintained in a secure, irreversible, anonymous and tamper-proof manner. Since the blockchain technology is decentralized, it makes the records public for every single entity in the node to view. A data block is added to the existing digital blockchain every time a new transaction is made.

When one person transfers money or any information to another person who is a part of the network, this new transaction will be added to the blockchain with a "specific code." This process is completely trustable because the blockchain shows every single transaction that happens in the network and if there is any data discrepancy or forging or stealing that happens, it can be identified easily.

What is The Big Deal About Decentralization?

The elimination of the third party during transactions has shown benefits in many ways. Most of the time, banks or government bodies often slow down the free flow of transactions due to time constraints – the amount of time taken to process the legal requirements and money transactions is more. But if blockchain technology were implemented, it would help people or businesses to trade more often in an efficient manner leading to an increase in international and local trade markets. The other important "headache" we often face with banks are the "expensive transaction fees" which is charged for transactions or money withdrawal. When it comes to blockchain technology, there is no transaction fee, and the security level is also on the higher side.

If blockchain technology gets into action in 'full mode,' then industries that rely on intermediaries will have to face extreme disruption.

How Does Blockchain Technology Work?

Instead of having a traditional central database (the banks, accountants or the government authorities), blockchain will act as a decentralized database (distributed ledger), which keeps updating all the digital records (transactions). This decentralized database is synchronized via the Internet with a network of replicated databases, which is visible to everyone within the connected network. These networks can work as a private network or public network depending on the requirement.

Whenever a transaction happens in the network, it is grouped into a block, which is protected by a cryptographic code and sent to the entire network every ten minutes based on the transaction flow. The miners (the people who spend their time and computational power) will be competing to validate these transactions by solving the complex cryptographic codes, and the first miner to solve the problem and validate the block will receive a reward.

These validated blocks are time-stamped and appended to the existing blockchain in linear chronological order. Every new block of transactions is attached to the older blocks that resemble a chain of blocks showing every single transaction that has been made in the history of that blockchain. This chain is continuously updated ensuring every single ledger in the network matches that in turn help each member to prove their ownership at any given point in time.

This technology helps in improving the trust factor and transacting peer to peer due to the transparent, cryptographic and decentralized model. The most common and dangerous threat every bank or government authorized body face nowadays is "hacking" as all these regulatory bodies have a large centralized database to control their regulatory process. This is completely impossible in blockchain technology. Let us try to understand this as an example.

> *If the hacker is looking to hack a particular block in the blockchain, he will have to hack the previous blocks to reach his specific intended block. But to hack the previous block, he will need to go back to its previous block leading to the necessity of hacking all the preceding blocks in the entire blockchain which means he will have to hack every single ledger in the network which can easily count to millions.*

A quick snapshot of the blockchain technology work-cycle:

Step by step guide on how this works:

- A transaction request is made

- This request is broadcasted to the P2P (peer to peer) network

- The transaction is validated by the nodes by using known algorithms

- Once the transaction is verified, it is combined with the other transactions to create a new data block for the ledger. (Cryptocurrency, contracts or other information would be involved in a verified transaction)

- This new verified block is added to the current blockchain making it permanently unalterable.

- The transaction request is now complete.

Pros and Cons of This Technology

Pros:

- Can be tracked accurately

- Acts as a permanent ledger

- Reduced cost

- More transparent

Cons:

- Challenges in implementation

- Regulatory implications

- Lot of competing platforms

- Too much complexity in understanding the technology

Potential applications where blockchain technology can be used

The security benefits and increased trust factor involved in this technology helps in using the blockchain technology in various application services.

- Financial services

You can save billions of dollars from the transaction costs in this faster mode of settlement service used by blockchain technology. It is not only fast but also transparent to everyone in the network.

- Healthcare services

This technology can also be used in the healthcare domain, which can help in sharing the patient's health records in an encrypted format to multiple providers without the risk of privacy breaches.

- Automotive industry

This technology can help consumers in managing fractional ownership of autonomous cars using the blockchain.

- Voting

The blockchain technology can efficiently determine the future of democracy. The constituents can cast their votes through a smartphone, computer or tablets using a blockchain code resulting in immediate results that are 'verified.'

From a business perspective, you can think of blockchain technology as the "improved next-generation business process software." The cost of trust can significantly offer higher returns for each dollar spent when compared to the traditional internal investments. Most of the industries, especially the financial industry, are exploring to use the blockchain technology to append everything from clearing settlements to insurance.

Will blockchain become the new Internet?

Definitely yes! This highly groundbreaking technology is going to change the world of Internet and revolutionize the global economy. The blockchain is becoming the "Internet of value" which enables us to exchange assets in an instant.

When this new technology completely takes its place in the global economy, the giant intermediaries will start facing a major setback as in blockchain; the trust factor is established via complex cryptographic code and consensus and not by placing your trust on the "central intermediary bodies."

The blockchain technology doesn't stop with money transfers and digital currencies but has more things to it, such as, patients' health record maintenance in the healthcare industry, property assets which are digitally recorded, electronic voting, small contracts and digital contents with proof of ownership.

Finance, banking, insurance, real estate, healthcare, legal sector, academic sector and public sectors are the major areas where intermediaries play a vital role.

Once blockchain has its full-fledged implementation in these areas, there will be complete transformation resulting in job losses. But the elimination of intermediate bodies will mostly bring positive benefits. The potential impact of this technology gains importance in the global economy as well as in the society.

Chapter Three: Bitcoin

The last two chapters would have helped you to understand the concept of cryptocurrency and the functionality of the blockchain technology, which is the underlying concept behind cryptocurrencies. We shall now try to understand about the first and the most popular cryptocurrency in the market – Bitcoin.

This digital currency is created and held electronically but is not printed like the fiat currencies (dollars, pounds, etc.). People use a software application, which solves cryptographic puzzles and also helps in increasing the businesses, produce Bitcoins. They can be traded in the digital world.

The most important feature of Bitcoin is that it is completely decentralized which means no particular organizational body can control its network. Bitcoins are mined in a distributed network using computing power and this also verifies the processed transactions made in the digital world thereby making it its payment network.

What is Bitcoin?

Bitcoin, otherwise known as the 'virtual gold,' is the world's first cryptocurrency, which distinguishes itself from its predecessors due to its "decentralization concept." Bitcoin can be referred to virtual currency or 'a reference to the blockchain technology.' The transactions can be made by wiring, cash or checks.

Bitcoin also referred BTC, can be used to refer a purchaser to your signature (security code encrypted with 16 distinct symbols) who will, in turn, decode the signature to get your cryptocurrency.

To make it simple, Bitcoin is the money which you can have in your online wallet to serve as an 'exchange medium' without a third-party intervention (banks, government-authorized body, etc.). The transactions happen directly based on the electronic peer-to-peer system.

What Is It Based On?

The conventional currency that is in use today is based on silver or gold. As per theory, when you hand over money to the bank, you are entitled to get some amount of gold that is equivalent to the money's value (though this is not in practice now). But Bitcoin is not based on gold or silver but is based on "pure mathematics."

You can produce new Bitcoins by using specific software programs that work on mathematical formula or puzzle. This particular mathematical formula is available on the Internet for free, and anyone across the world can check it. It is an open source software application.

As per the original specification, only 21 million Bitcoins can be created, which means you cannot keep producing Bitcoins 'for like forever,' so inflation will never be a problem. But there is a chance of deflation to happen in the Bitcoin's world where there might be a reduction in the price of goods or services in the global economy.

How Does It Work?

Let us understand this in both functional and technical level:

Functional level:

A distributed public ledger called blockchain is found on the Bitcoin network. This ledger maintains the record of every single transaction that has ever happened in that particular network.

Whenever a new transaction request is made, the transaction is checked for its validity and then confirmed. Once the transaction is verified, Bitcoins are rewarded. The verification process is done by the 'miners,' and the process is referred to as 'mining.' Each transaction's authenticity is secured by digital signatures that correspond to the sending addresses thereby allowing all the users in the network to have control over sending the Bitcoins.

Any user can verify the transactions through the process of mining and get rewarded with Bitcoins.

Technical level:

You will need to install a Bitcoin wallet on your system or mobile. Once the installation is done, it will initiate your first Bitcoin address. This address can be given to your friends to start payment transactions. This is similar to your email IDs, but in this case, the Bitcoin address can be used only once. The entire Bitcoin network works on blockchain technology, which means all the transactions that are confirmed will be included in the blockchain.

What is a transaction? The transfer of value between the Bitcoin wallets is called transaction, and this value is what gets appended to the blockchain. A secret piece of data called seed or the private key is kept in the Bitcoin wallet. This seed or private key is used to sign the transactions with a "mathematical proof." This is to ensure that the owner indeed sends the information. The digital signature stops the transaction from getting breached once it is issued.

All the transactions are broadcasted between the users in the network, and the confirmation is done in ten minutes (by the miner). Mining is the process by which all the pending transactions are confirmed and appended to the blockchain. Chronological order is imposed in the blockchain to help in protecting the neutrality of the network thereby allowing the different nodes (computers) to agree on the system's process.

Verification can be done only through strict cryptographic rules, which pack all the pending transactions into a block, which is then appended to the existing blockchain. Once a transaction is confirmed, it cannot be reversed.

How to Buy a Bitcoin?

Beginners can use broker apps, such as blockchain or CoinBase, to buy the cryptocurrency 'Bitcoin'. These apps will allow the user to use their plastic money (debit card or credit card) to exchange 'fiat currency' for Bitcoin.

There is no compulsion to buy the entire Bitcoins, but it can be purchased based on the cash investment value (i.e., if the user has 20000 dollars, he can purchase Bitcoins worth the said value). The miners will then verify and approve the request made. Once the approval is done, the money will be debited from the user's plastic money account in exchange for the Bitcoin. In case the user wants to sell the Bitcoins he had purchased, he can use the same app and sell their Bitcoins in return for the Bitcoin's cash value.

Instead of going through a broker app, one can also buy the Bitcoin straight from the respective merchants on other sites; however, the procedure is more complicated and risky. Bitcoins can also be bought by depositing cash at Bitcoin ATM's. To find the location of the Bitcoin ATM, you can use Coin ATM radar or directly Google it out.

Things to be done before purchasing a Bitcoin

The following things are to be done before you decide to buy a Bitcoin:

- Install a virtual wallet (Bitcoin wallet) onto your mobile or computer. This wallet keeps track of all your transactions and Bitcoin balance.

- You will need to deposit the "real money" via an online payment company or transfer from your bank account to a third party website's bank account. This third party website will connect all the Bitcoin buyers and sellers.

- When your funds are ready, you can place an order for Bitcoin through cryptocurrency exchanges such as 'Bitstamp' (the process works similar to tradition stock exchange)

- You can also purchase Bitcoins from third parties like BitInstant who will take the responsibility of directly sending the Bitcoins to your virtual wallet.

Places To Find Bitcoins

You can buy your first Bitcoins from any of these places:

- Bitcoin ATM (change cash or Bitcoins for another cryptocurrency), E.g., BTER, CoinCorner

- Cryptocurrency exchange (exchange money for Bitcoins), E.g., CoinBase, LocalBitcoins, BitBargain, Bittylicious, BuyUCoin, Zebpay

- Trusted service that helps you to find a seller for trading Bitcoins for cash. E.g., LocalBitcoins

- You can also sell a service or product for Bitcoins. E.g., Purse (website)

Bitcoin and Its Characteristics

There are many important features that set Bitcoin aside and differentiate it from the traditional currencies. Let us look at the functional or transactional properties of Bitcoins:

Decentralized setup

It doesn't have a single central authority to be controlled. Every single node (computer) that processes the transaction and mines the Bitcoin becomes a part of the network enabling all the connected nodes to work together using P2P (peer to peer) network. The money keeps flowing even if a part of the network goes down at every single node in the network has the distributed ledger to track information.

Quick and easy to structure

You don't need to stand in queues, fill those long application forms, and submit the KYC documents to open an account. Bitcoin address can be generated within seconds with no extra charges.

Anonymity

Users can have multiple Bitcoin addresses without the need to be linked with their personal information, such as name, address or anything related to personal identification.

Transparency

The distributed ledger (blockchain) stores and maintains the details of all the transactions that have happened in the network. If you are using a public Bitcoin address, everyone in the network will know your Bitcoin count, but the catch is they won't know it is yours.

If you do not want too much transparency in your transactional activity, you can keep changing your Bitcoin address often or by not transferring too many Bitcoins to a particular address consistently.

Miniscule transaction fee

The bank transaction fee for the transaction that happens from your bank account to other bank accounts or international bank accounts will be on a higher end, but with Bitcoin, there is almost no transaction fee.

Fast and reliable

Once the Bitcoin network confirms and accepts the transactions, you can send money anywhere at any point in time and will not need to wait for banking hours. It is fast, and the money arrives within minutes.

Non-repudiable

When you send your Bitcoins, you cannot get them back unless the recipient returns them to you. They are gone forever.

Is There a Way to Store the Bitcoins?

By now you are aware that Bitcoins can be stored in a virtual wallet known as the cryptocurrency wallet (Bitcoin wallet in this case). You can choose to use any of the below mentioned three applications of the Bitcoin wallet:

Full client

You can control the whole transaction process all by yourself without using a third-party service. This is similar to a standalone email server. But this will not suit beginners, as it is too complicated.

Lightweight client

You can use a third party owned server to access the Bitcoin network and perform the transactions. This is similar to a standalone mail client who will need to connect to a mail server for accessing its mailbox.

Web client

A third party will take control of the entire transaction process where you will only be a user. This is similar to your webmail that entirely relies on a third party server.

How to Buy and Sell Things Using Bitcoin?

By now you will have understood that Bitcoins are not real money which you can touch and feel like your fiat currencies such as dollars, yen, euros, pounds, etc. There are only records of transactions that have happened between different addresses with the increase and decrease in Bitcoins balance. These details are updated in the distributed ledger (blockchain).

In such cases, how do we do the buying and selling using this cryptocurrency? Let us understand this using an example.

Sam wants to buy an electronic gadget from Alisha using his Bitcoin. He will be sending her the following:

- Private key

- Sequence of numbers or letters (This private data will hold the details of Alisha's digital wallet address, amount, his source transaction of the coins)

- Address (This will have public sequence of numbers and letters)

Alisha will decode the private key with her smartphone by scanning it. At this moment, all the other participants (nodes) of the network will receive a broadcast of Sam's transaction request on their ledger. In the next ten minutes, the request gets confirmed through the process called 'mining.' This process will let Alisha know if she can go ahead with Sam's transaction or not.

How to Protect Your Bitcoins?

Following the below mentioned four steps might help you to protect your Bitcoins:

- Store only small amounts of Bitcoins on your mobile or personal computer for everyday use and place the remaining Bitcoins in a safer environment.

- For better security, keep some of your Bitcoins in an offline environment that is disconnected from your network. This is similar to your normal routine with money, like how you would only keep a required amount in your wallet and leave the rest in the bank or at home.

- Ensure you keep updating your system software regularly to avoid getting attacked by viruses or malware. If you would want to be extra cautious and careful about your Bitcoins, then try using Bitcoins' multi-signature feature, which will require multiple independent approvals for a transaction to happen.

- Ensure you take a backup of your wallet at regular intervals and encrypt your digital wallet or smartphone with a strong password to protect it from getting stolen.

NanoLedger S and KeepKey are the two hardware wallets that can be used.

Disadvantages of Bitcoin

The complexity of the Bitcoin software and the currency's volatility discourage many from using it. Sometimes the transactions can be too slow which can frustrate the users. Reddit users had recently reported that they had to wait for close to an hour to get their transactions confirmed.

You need to watch out for these four Bitcoin scams:

- Bitcoin Exchange scams

- Bitcoin Mining scams

- Ponzi scams

- Bitcoin Wallet scams

Quick help to get into action mode

After reading through this chapter, do you think you are ready to explore this new digital currency? You can browse through the following websites to find wallets, check on the stores that accept Bitcoins, the exchanges that help in trading Bitcoins and more news or guidelines about this cryptocurrency.

- Blockchain.info (helps to check transactions on the ledger, such as, checking how much money you have in your wallet, how many BTC is stored in a particular wallet address, etc.)

- Bitcoin.org (helps to choose your Bitcoin wallet)

- 99Bitcoins (tutorial which explains how to buy Bitcoins using plastic money)

- Buy Bitcoin Worldwide (helps to find a Bitcoin exchange)

- Weusecoins.com (contains a list of exchanges to help trade Bitcoins worldwide).

Chapter Four: Mining

The government prints our traditional money as authorized bodies as and when there is a need, but in the case of Bitcoin, this does not happen as Bitcoin cannot be printed which you will have understood by now.

Bitcoin is created digitally using computers. Bitcoins are mined across the world using specific software by solving complex mathematical puzzles. This process is called mining and the people who mine the coins are called miners.

How Does This Entire Process Happen?

Bitcoins are being sent across the Bitcoin network almost all the time and it is crucial to keep track of the record of these transactions to know who paid what and to whom. This is dealt with by collecting all these transactions and packing them into a block in the Bitcoin network. These 'blocks' are then verified to have the transaction confirmed by the miners who writes them to the distributed ledger.

Hash Algorithm

The distributed ledger, which is a long chain of blocks otherwise referred to as blockchain is used to check the transactions made between the Bitcoin addresses in the network. As and when a new block of transaction takes place, this keeps adding to the existing blockchain creating a lengthy list of all the transactions that have ever taken place in the Bitcoin network. The block is constantly updated keeping the participants aware of whatever is going on in the network.

To ensure these transactions are not tampered with, a complex process known as mining takes place and the miners hold the entire responsibility for the same. A maths formula is applied to the block, which turns the original message into a random series of words and letters called as a hash. The hash then gets stored at the end of the blockchain alongside the block at that time.

Producing a hash from a collection of data is easy but working out what the data was by looking at the hash is impossible as each hash is unique. In case you change one character in a Bitcoin block, then the entire hash will change.

Each block's hash is produced with the hash of its previous block that confirms that the block and the preceding blocks are legitimate. This is something similar to a wax seal.

When you try changing the block to fake a transaction, the hash automatically gets changed and when the block's authenticity is checked by running the hashing algorithm on the said block, it can be easily identified that the current hash is different from the already stored one in the blockchain which would instantly spot it as 'forged'.

Mining Bitcoins

Miners compete with each other to 'stamp' the block as mentioned above using the software that is specifically written to mine these blocks. Whenever a miner gets successful in creating a hash, he is rewarded with Bitcoins and every other participant in the network gets to hear about this. Generating a hash from the collection of data can be easily done with computers but what makes it difficult in the Bitcoin network is the concept of "proof of work."

This protocol will not accept just any old hash, but the block's hash should adhere to certain formats – must have a specific number of zeroes in the beginning. You will have no idea what the hash is going to look like before you generate it. Meddling with the transaction data in the block will create complete havoc during hash creation. If the already created hash has to be changed due to the change in the data, then it is done through another random piece of data known as 'nonce.' In case the hash doesn't adhere to the required format then the nonce is changed to make the whole block hashed again.

The challenge that every miner will undergo is finding how the nonce (proof of work) works and this is the most complicated process for which the miners will be competing with each other, and that is how their rewarding happens.

What is Bitcoin Mining?

Bitcoin mining is a computational process in a decentralized network that has two purposes:

- Confirming transactions with dedicated computational power and by devoting the required 'time' to the block

- Generating new Bitcoins in each block

The protocol that makes this entire process complicated is the "proof of work." This costs the computing power that is translated to time, energy and hardware utilization.

It works in the following manner:

- A new block is proposed

- This block is combined with the hash and nonce

- It checks if the hash number is less than the target value.

- If yes, the 'proof of work' is solved

- If no, the nonce is incremented, and the hash is created again to check if the hash number is less than the target value

- The process continues until the 'proof of work' is solved. If the POW (proof of work) is solved, then the miner gets his reward in the form of Bitcoins.

Determine the Target Value is Where the Mining Difficulty Lies.

Bitcoin mining is designed to be difficult and resource-specific to ensure there is a steady rate of mining the number of blocks. The proof of work plays a major role to ensure each block is valid and is verified by other nodes in the network every time a new block is received. Bitcoin mining is similar to 'gold mining' as it requires immense strain from the miners that gradually makes this cryptocurrency available at a rate similar to the gold rate in the market.

Proof of Work

'Hashcash' is the 'proof of work' function used in Bitcoin. This piece of data is time-consuming to generate, as it needs to satisfy specific criteria in the protocol. It is important to check if the data is adhering to the said requirements. By the time the proof of work is generated, the miners would have had multiple attempts to ensure the "valid proof of work" is produced.

This can be considered as a random process with very little probability that requires a lot of trial and error method before getting the required output.

Bitcoin Mining Difficulty

The SHA-256 hash of a block's header should be equal to or lower than the target value for the block to be accepted by the network. Since the hash of the block must start with a specific number of zeroes, calculating the probability of hash in a way such that it starts with the mentioned number of zeroes is too minimal leading to the miners having to make multiple attempts. Every time a new hash is generated, the nonce needs to be incremented.

When more miners compete in the network, the block creation value goes up leading to decrease in the average time taken to mine. This results in mining difficulty. When the mining difficulty is more, the block creation value decreases, which makes the average time taken to mine to 'normal mode,' and the cycle continues. The ideal average mining time is stabilized to "ten minutes per block."

Bitcoin Mining Hardware Used by Miners

There are various Bitcoin mining hardware available on the market, and these are the few most popularly used ones:

- Avalon6

- Antminer S9

- Antminer S7

- Antminer S5

- Antminer R4

- Sp20 Jackson

- ASIC Bitcoin miner (Application Specific Integrated Circuits)

Bitcoin Cloud Mining

When you use Bitcoin mining hardware devices to perform the mining activities, you will have to spend a lot of electricity, manage the heat generated from the device and other maintenance issues. To provide a solution for these issues, cloud hashing or cloud mining was introduced.

Miners can purchase the mining capacity of hardware in datacenters and can earn their Bitcoins without the need to manage and maintain the hardware devices. This is because all the Bitcoin mining happens in the cloud. When the Bitcoin mining is done in the cloud, the miners can keep themselves away with issues rising concerning heat, electricity, installation, maintenance and various other hosting problems.

Advantages

The advantages which one gets to enjoy in this cloud mining are:

- It avoids electricity costs.

- Can work in peace without getting disturbed by the sound of constant whirring fans in the hardware.

- No necessity to deal with excess heat problems.

- No need to worry about ventilation issues.

Disadvantages

Bitcoin cloud mining seems to be having more disadvantages than advantages:

- Bitcoin cloud mining can be shady as they are not from verified sources.

- Tend to get bored, as you don't get to build your own Bitcoin hashing systems.

- Get lower profits, as the cloud mining operator expenses are more.

- Can be fraudulent.

- Ability to stop payouts or operations in the Bitcoin mining contracts.

- Won't be able to change the Bitcoin mining software.

Chapter Five: Trading and Investing in Cryptocurrency

By now, you will have clarity on cryptocurrency and the famous buzzwords 'blockchain' and 'Bitcoins.' Now that you have understood the detailing involved in this new technology, it is time to get to the crux of the show. Since cryptocurrency has already started to make its mark as the new digital currency in the market, we need to understand the trading and investing options available for the same.

What is the difference between trading and investing? Trading in cryptocurrency means 'to swap cryptocurrencies' via online exchanges. This is similar to forex currency trading. Investing in cryptocurrency means buying a particular cryptocurrency and waiting for its price value to increase so that you can sell the same for profit.

How to start? Are there any helpful resources? What are the things to be taken care of? With people becoming more and more aware of the current technology trending in the market, they take an equal amount of effort and time to get to know the new 'hit in the market' and never hesitate to 'try out the same.'

Though Bitcoin is the first popular cryptocurrency in the market, there are equally more numbers of new cryptocurrencies that have made its mark in the digital market. They claim to be better than Bitcoin in many ways and are competing to carve a niche for themselves. The other cryptocurrencies are referred in general as 'altcoins.' These altcoins are attaining market value in quick speed and are taking all the necessary steps to crumble down the market capital value of Bitcoin.

Cryptocurrencies You Can Buy

There are thousands of cryptocurrencies available in the market for you to invest or trade with. But which is the best option? Bitcoin and Ethereum are the two popular currencies that top the chart. You can also try LiteCoin.

Risks and Regulations

The current market volatility is the most important thing to look out when you decide to invest or trade in cryptocurrencies. The risk value is high mostly due to security alerts involved in digital wallets. Wallets and offline marketplaces are often the targets for hackers, as people tend to store their valuable Bitcoins in either of these places.

Market volatility is highly unpredictable as it depends on the 'sudden decline in the value of fiat currencies.'

Digital Wallet

Digital wallet can help in storing anything from data to information. It is completely digitized using codes. One can store cryptocurrencies or any information in these wallets as it works similar to your 'normal wallet' where you store your money or coins along with much of other information like cards, notes, keys, etc.

There are two types of digital wallet:

- Hot wallet

These digital wallets can be used online using mobile apps for trading, selling and buying purposes.

- Cold wallet

These digital wallets are used in an offline mode where you can link your cryptocurrency addresses to your own digital address and store them online in an external storage device.

Both these wallets come with security risk factor, as they are viable to hacking. Since hot wallets work online, they are prone to get hacked easily if proper care is not taken. One can lose information in the cold wallet if the external storage device or the hard disks that are used to store these wallets are not maintained securely.

Cryptocurrency Wallets (Online)

One can use the inbuilt wallets given by the exchanges or choose to have their own hardware wallets. Go for a paper wallet services (myetherwallet.com) or spend some amount of money on choosing hardware wallets like KeepKey.

If you had already been storing your cryptocurrencies in exchange and would like to look at a long-term storage option, you can check out the following steps to transfer the cryptocurrencies to your hardware wallet:

- Get your KeepKey USB cable plugged
- Choose the 'KeepKey Client' option in the 'apps' menu in Google Chrome
- Search for your wallet address on the KeepKey Client user interface.
- You will need to access the 'Send/Request' tab in the Coinbase exchange

- Enter your KeepKey wallet address
- Click 'Send Funds' once you have confirmed the amount to be transferred.

The above steps help in transferring cryptocurrencies from the inbuilt wallet of Coinbase exchange to the hardware wallet KeepKey. To be on a safer side, try sending a minimum amount and check if it is working to avoid unnecessary network fees just in case you encounter an error or lose the amount transferred.

How to Make a Bitcoin Purchase Using Cryptocurrency Exchange?

If you want to buy or sell your cryptocurrencies using fiat money, then you will have to go through cryptocurrency exchange. Before you decide on the exchange, which is suitable for you, ensure you check the quality and reliability of the exchange. It should be user-friendly, should have complete details on withdrawal and purchase limits, transaction fees (if any), insurance, security, liquidity flow and trading volume.

Coinbase is said to be the most user-friendly exchange with cent percent crypto insurance. Once you have your functional bank account ready and your details verified in CoinBase, you could get your Bitcoin purchase done using the following steps:

- Click on the 'Buy/Sell Bitcoin tab.'
- Using the drop-down menu, choose your mode of payment
- Type the required amount

- Click on the 'Buy Bitcoin instantly' button
- To check if your Bitcoins have been credited, view your dashboard on the exchange.

One more important thing to note before you decide your exchange is - to check its ease of withdrawal and funding activities in case you are using currencies apart from USD.

How to Start Trading?

Once you get familiar with buying cryptocurrencies and would like to explore the trading options, you can use GDAX as your trading platform. Transfer from Coinbase to GDAX is instant and is also free of charge. You can compare CoinBase as a 'place where you can buy and store the cryptocurrencies' and GDAX as 'the related trading platform.'

You can start exploring other exchanges such as Polo, Bittrex, etc. once you start getting familiar with various other cryptocurrencies in the market. But there are few important things to be taken care of while signing up as a new user:

- Ensure you verify your account with all the required documents at the early stage itself

- In case you skip this step, then you might end up getting caught up with certain tedious and slow administrative works at a later stage

- It may take days to get the details verified in the exchange, so it is better to get it done in the beginning to avoid the risk of losing trading opportunities when the market is at its peak.

- Only when you trade, will you find a gradual increase in the purchase and withdrawal limits.

Steps to Get Started:

- You will need to create a digital wallet to store your cryptocurrency in a secured manner for which you will have to sign up with coinbase.com

- To exchange the cryptocurrency with fiat money, you will need to connect your plastic money (credit or debit card) or bank account.

- Buy a cryptocurrency to start the process.

- Sell the cryptocurrency which you just bought when the time is right

- Get signed up to another 'exchange' to trade your existing cryptocurrency with another cryptocurrency.

- Once you have successfully traded the new cryptocurrency, bring it back to CoinBase and then convert it to back to fiat money.

Let us understand the above steps with an example:

"You buy Bitcoin (BTC) using your currency USD (through bank transfer) and then wait for the right trading opportunity. Once you see the market stocks going up, you sell the Bitcoin (BTC) using the exchange 'CoinBase' and get the fiat currency (USD).

After this, you sign up with another exchange for trading Bitcoin (BTC) with Ethereum (ETH). Use the USD and buy Ethereum (ETH). Then put it back to CoinBase and again sell the same for the fiat currency (USD) based on the market value.

In case you had spent $10 for buying Bitcoin (BTC) and got $20 while selling it; then again you used that $20 to buy Ethereum (ETH) for $15 and then you again sold the Ethereum (ETH) for $35 thereby making a profit of $25."

Things to be Taken Care of While Trading:

Please ensure you take extra care by following the below-mentioned steps while trading with cryptocurrencies.

- Always choose a reputed company that helps in offering the exchange and wallet with the easy user interface and a definitely secured environment.

- Choose cryptocurrencies such as Bitcoin, Ethereum, and Litecoins which are prominently used in the market instead of risking with new cryptocurrencies

- Start by mastering CoinBase (for purchase and selling) and GDAX (for trading) before trying your hand with other exchanges such as binance, Kraken, Bittrex, etc.

- Get into 'trading coins' only if you understand the tax implications clearly, else it is always good to stick to 'trading fiat currencies with cryptocurrencies'

- Both Coinbase and GDAX would be requesting for a lot of personal information so be ready for the same as these broker apps are the trusted ones which provides the platform for buyers and sellers to meet in the digital world without worrying too much about the risk factor.

- It is better to use your bank account than using your plastic money.

- It will take minimum 3 to 5 days for your bank account to get paired with your exchange.

- Adhere to your purchase or buying limits

- If you trade more, your trading fee goes down.

- Keep your exchange and wallet secure by following two-factor authentication

- Bitcoins cost more since 2017, which makes the users choose other cryptocurrencies. But not to worry, you don't need to buy the full coin; you can always purchase a fraction of it based on your budget.

- Use your mobile as it is quicker and easier when you download the app.

- You can try setting up alerts to inform you on the 'ups and downs of the market value' to help you decide when to trade

Top Five Mistakes to Avoid

As a new trader, it is best to know the mistakes that need to be avoided to ensure you don't suffer a nervous breakdown

Don't fall for the wrong 'exchange.'

There are many cryptocurrency exchanges in the market as the number of altcoins keeps growing at an enormous rate. It is always wise to choose the 'well known established exchanges' and trade using 'established cryptocurrencies.' Once your cryptocurrency is gone, it will be impossible to reclaim it from unknown exchange companies. It is said that – "Known devil is always better than an unknown angel."

Don't get nervous

When it comes to trading irrespective of your normal trading or cryptocurrency trading, it is important to 'not get nervous.' Decisions taken in fear and panic will lead to disastrous results. Especially when it comes to cryptocurrency market, as it is extremely volatile. Watch the market, think, trust your gut instinct and then decide.

Don't take 'too much time.'

When you spend way too much time in deciding, you might end up losing amazing opportunity to see profits. Getting glued to the market sites, looking at the market fluctuations and taking more than the needed time to decide, will lead to exhaustion as you might have lost a good profit since you took more than a day to trust your gut instinct.

Don't get your hands on 'many cryptocurrencies at the same time.'

It is good to try to make profits with two or more cryptocurrencies but do it only if you are familiar with at least one cryptocurrency before taking a plunge to handle more than you actually can. Get into research mode; choose the coins that are popularly known for their trading volumes and steady market capital.

Don't tumble into scams

Don't get into 'excited mode' when you see new altcoins in the market which is claiming to show an extensive profit in short period of time. It might be a scam. Avoid trading with altcoins that can be traded only within the company's closed system as the value can be manipulated than its actual worth.

How Much to Invest?

The volatility in the market value makes cryptocurrency highly unpredictable, but at the same time, it can give you the possibility to write your own 'rags to riches' story if you can take control over your emotional senses and think logically at the right time. The first important thing you need to keep as an 'underlying factor in your head' is being ready 'to put only the amount of money which you are okay to lose without going through an emotional turmoil.' Example, if you don't bother to lose your $50 which you are going to invest in cryptocurrency, then go with $50 rather than spending $500.

Try out your cryptocurrency investments in the following percentage:

- If you are less than 30 years old, then go for 50% traditional investments and 30% cryptocurrency investments

- If you fall between the age criteria (30 to 40 years), then 60% traditional investments and 20% cryptocurrency investments may do good

- If you are above 40 years old, go for 70% traditional investments and only 10% cryptocurrency investments.

These need not be taken as hard and fast rules as it can always differ from person to person. Age constraint is taken into consideration as one's financial responsibilities go up based on the age.

How to Invest?

The best way to invest in cryptocurrency is first to buy some. You can buy Bitcoins or other altcoins using the cryptocurrency exchange. Coinbase – the most commonly used exchange; can help the customers by selling their Bitcoins at 1% markup in the market rate. It also allows you to link your bank account to your wallet for making transfers easier and faster.

Coinbase also provides an 'automatic buy order' option which enables you to keep buying Bitcoins for a particular rate on a monthly basis automatically. But the disadvantage of this service is you will not be able to have control of the price at which the Bitcoins are bought, and it may sometimes exceed your budget too.

Bitstamp – another traditional Bitcoin exchange; can help you indirectly interacting with the other Bitcoin users thereby increasing the liquidity value. You can also look at buying Bitcoins offline using 'Local Bitcoins.' Choose the best platform for your investment based on your needs and comfort, be it CoinBase or BitStamp or Local Bitcoins.

Once you have Bitcoins or altcoins in your wallet and have got yourself into 'investment or trading mode,' have a hawk's eye in the market and sell them for fiat currencies or trade them at the right time.

Don't hesitate to follow the famous proverb – "Make hay while the sun shines."

About the Author

James F Parker graduated from Duke University with an MBA degree in Finance. He now lives in Vancouver as an entrepreneur and works part time as a consultant at an Information Technology firm.

It is his life's mission to educate and assist others in building a more secure future for themselves and their families by continuously providing up to date information and ensuring they stay on track with their goals.

While Bitcoin was still at its infancy, he was introduced to his mentor who specialized in crypto assets. In 2011, James transitioned to focus mainly on cryptocurrency after following the revolutionary technology and gaining special interest in its potential to become the new future of finance.

After several years and pioneering numerous startups, James continues to build his portfolio and investments surrounding the blockchain technology while improving and learning about this fascinating topic.

As an entrepreneur, James has founded several online and offline businesses, and launched many open-sourced projects.

Armed with extensive knowledge in the new form of a worldwide payment system, he wants to share all his learnings (and failures) about this new form of currency to assist others in gaining a better life through passive income.

Before You Go...

We have come to the end of this book. I hope the information wasn't too heavy to understand but instead gave you an interesting read. This book would have helped you with an overview of blockchain technology, its uses and a basic guide on how to mine, trade and invest in cryptocurrency.

I sincerely hope this book was useful and has helped in answering most of your queries you had in mind. My best wishes to you for making the best out of the cryptocurrency market to help you in increasing your financial strength for good.

DID YOU FIND VALUE IN THIS BOOK?

YES? PLEASE LET ME KNOW BY LEAVING AN HONEST REVIEW ON AMAZON. I would sincerely appreciate your time and consideration. As you may already be aware, reviews are incredibly crucial to the success of any author and I truly welcome all words and ratings.

NO? PLEASE ALSO LET ME KNOW! Email me at jamesfparker1@gmail.com and let me know what it was that you did not like. I highly encourage reaching out to me this way as I take all comments seriously and would love to improve my book to provide the most value to everyone. Help me serve you better!

Thank you and good luck!